CW00661757

NOW F**K OFF!

THE LITTLE GUIDE TO
SUCCESSION

First published in 2024 by OH
An Imprint of HEADLINE PUBLISHING GROUP

2 4 6 8 10 9 7 5 3 1

Disclaimer:

ISBN 978-1-80069-633-4

Compiled and written by: Malcolm Croft
Editorial: Victoria Denne
Designed and typeset in Avenir by: Andy Jones
Project manager: Russell Porter
Production: Marion Storz
Printed and bound in China

HEADLINE PUBLISHING GROUP
An Hachette UK Company
Carmelite House, 50 Victoria Embankment, London EC4Y 0DZ

www.headline.co.uk   www.hachette.co.uk

NOW F**K OFF!

THE LITTLE GUIDE TO
SUCCESSION

UNOFFICIAL AND UNAUTHORIZED

CONTENTS

INTRODUCTION - 6

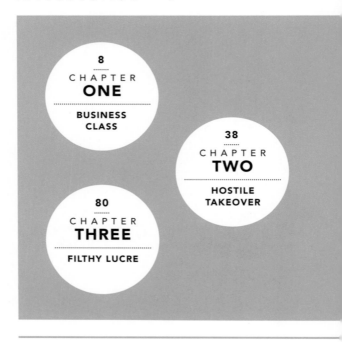

8

CHAPTER
ONE

BUSINESS
CLASS

38

CHAPTER
TWO

HOSTILE
TAKEOVER

80

CHAPTER
THREE

FILTHY LUCRE

114

CHAPTER
FOUR

ENEMIES
FOREIGN &
DOMESTIC

146

CHAPTER
FIVE

FLESH &
BLOOD

INTRODUCTION

Welcome to your one-stop shop for all things related to the shitshow at the fuck factory, or as we like to call it, *Succession*, the swear-friendly American family dramedy created by the genius-level mind of British TV writer Jesse Armstrong.

If your life today feels bereft of joy, titillation, and pleasure, it's because *Succession* – the most acclaimed TV show of the millennium so far – concluded its four-season lust for glory in 2023. Along the way, it gobbled up every major award going, as well as receiving universal acclaim from fans and critics. It became a rare example of a show that, like Waystar's finances, grew richer with each episode, while also ratcheting up its suspense and ruthlessness to near-ridiculous levels before its shock-twist conclusion. The show delivered on its intellectual property too – a riches-to-even-more-riches tale of ripping the Roy family to ribbons, all in the quest to find the right-sized head to fit the crown – like *Game of Thrones*, in many ways, if the Lannisters wore $10,000-dollar suits. And while there will sadly be no more adventures of the Roys and their motley crew of Royco executives, there is enough wit, wisdom, and wizardry in the 39 episodes we have to ensure the show's legacy lives on long after the hyperbole has fossilized.

The Little Guide to Succession is essential reading for fans of the show, a tiny tome dressed to impress with all the quickfire quips, perspicacious profanity, and outstanding one-liners we all now happily deploy daily to sound much cleverer than we are, proof of the show's wicked way of weaponizing words to wonderful effect. Of course, as is to be expected, this celebratory compendium contains quite a lot of cursing, so be warned. Thankfully, all of it is awesome.

Now, with that in mind, let us leave this introduction with the wise words of Logan Roy: "Meeting over. Now fuck off."

CHAPTER ONE

BUSINESS CLASS

Greed. Betrayal. Tragedy. Rivalry. Lust. Power. Awkward displays of affection. *Succession* has it all. And so much more.

The show is pure 21st-century Shakespeare, complete with enough bawdry boardroom backstabbing to make the Bard spin back to life in his grave with joy. For the Roy family, as well as the wayward executives and minions of the Waystar Royco empire, the only thing that matters is the company you keep. Everything else is just business.

Speaking of which, let's get down to it…

Business is my fucking.

Kendall, *to Roman, making it clear to his brother what his priorities are – even at Tom's bachelor party.*

Season 1, Episode 8, "Prague".
Written by Jon Brown.

* "Okay, let's find you a Bloomberg terminal to stick your dick in," responds Roman.

You know, I know that you've read a lot of books about business management and this and that, but you know what? Sometimes, it is a big dick competition.

***Logan**, to Kendall, about how Kendall got "bent over and fucked" by Lawrence Yee, CEO of Vaulter, in his unwinnable quest to please his father.*

Season 1, Episode 1, "Celebration".
Written by Jesse Armstrong.

You're such fucking dopes. You're not serious figures. I love you, but you are not serious people.

Logan, *speaking candidly to Shiv, Roman and Kendall for the last time before his death, regarding the inheritance of the business, and the only time in the show when he tells his kids he actually loves them.*

Season 4, Episode 2, "Rehearsal".
Written by Tony Roche & Susan Soon He Stanton.

You can't make a Tomelette without breaking some Gregs.

Tom, to Greg (emailed to Greg 67 times by Tom in one evening, except between 3 a.m. and 5 a.m.) regarding the burning of the scandalous Brightstar Cruises sexual misconduct documents. Why Tom felt the need to send it 67 times was never explained.

Season 2, Episode 9, "DC".
Written by Jesse Armstrong.

I don't mean to be insulting, but, having been around a bit… my hunch is that you're going to get fucked. Because I've seen you get fucked a lot. And I've never seen Logan get fucked once.

Tom, *to Kendall, after Kendall tries to turn Tom against Logan during his hostile takeover of Waystar Royco. If Tom's in it to win it, this line proves it.*

Season 3, Episode 6, "What It Takes".
Written by Will Tracy.

3,021

The total number of times the word "fuck" is said throughout the show's four seasons. That's an average of 76 "fucks" per episode, or one every 1.2 minutes, and no less than 40 "fucks" per episode.

The Season 3 finale, "All the Bells Say", has the most "fucks" of any episode – 119!

* Roman Roy says "fuck" the most – 523 times.

Honestly, honey, it's like this 900-pound gorilla has finally stopped fucking me. **99**

Tom, *to Shiv, after Greg had disposed of the sexual misconduct documents relating to the Brightstar Cruises scandal which could implicate Tom if known, a fact that Shiv knew all too well.*

Season 1, Episode 6, "Which Side Are You On?'
Written by Susan Soon He Stanton.

"

You're a clumsy interloper, no one trusts you and the only guy pulling for you is dead. Now you're just married to the ex-boss's daughter, and she doesn't even like you. You are fairly, squarely fucked.

"

Karl, to Tom, when Tom "respectfully" threw his hat into the ring for interim CEO following the sudden death of Logan. Karl says it like he sees it but would ultimately be proved wrong.

Season 4, Episode 4, "Honeymoon States'.
Written by Jesse Armstrong & Lucy Prebble.

He's just moseying, terrifyingly moseying. He's wearing sunglasses inside. It looks like as if Santa Claus was a hitman. He's just walking around, but with the slight sense that he might kill someone. It's like *Jaws* if everyone in *Jaws* worked for Jaws.

Greg, *to a panicked Tom, after learning Logan will keep control of ATN per the terms of the GoJo sale and Logan's surprise drop-in at the ATN newsroom to announce his revamp for the channel's future.*

Season 4, Episode 2, "Rehearsal".
Written by Tony Roche & Susan Soon He Stanton.

> The script was sent to me to read for the character of Greg. I didn't feel like I clicked with that character, but I liked the script enough to continue reading. In the script Roman walks in the room and says, "Hey, hey, motherfuckers!" There was something that clicked with me and this character that's something I still don't understand, and probably don't want to understand, considering the kind of guy he is.

Kieran Culkin
Hollywood Reporter, _December 16, 2018._

You realize how fucked you're going to be as soon as you're of no use to him?

__Roman__, to a beaten Kendall, after Kendall is pulled out of a rehab facility in Iceland to give a public statement regarding his decision to back off from his role in Stewy and Sandy's hostile takeover. Roman and Shiv insult Kendall for being Logan's "sex robot for Dad to fuck".

Season 2, Episode 1, "The Summer Palace".
Written by Jesse Armstrong.

Do you know nothing of the company you're supposed to be taking over? You know, Waystar? Waystar Royco. We do hate speech and rollercoasters.

Roman, to Shiv, discussing the hostile takeover of the family business and Shiv's apparent lack of knowledge, foreshadowing Rhea Jarrell's fooling of Shiv – at Logan's request.

Season 2, Episode 7, "Return".
Written by Jonathan Glatzer.

You're a fucking beast.

Kendall, *to Logan, after Logan makes it clear that Kendall does not have what it takes to inherit the reins to Waystar Royco, calling him a "hothouse flower". Kendall's delivery of the line is spine-tingling.*

Season 1, Episode 10, "Nobody Is Ever Missing".
Written by Jesse Armstrong.

> **"** We'll fuckin' beast 'em. We'll go full fucking beast! **"**

__Logan__, becoming the "beast" Kendall always knew him to be, as the Roy siblings kickstart a civil war with Logan over the future of Waystar after Kendall's devastating press conference U-turn.

Season 3, Episode 1, "Secession".
Written by Jesse Armstrong.

The Logan Roy School of Journalism? What's next, the Jack the Ripper Women's Health Clinic?

__Ewan__, to Greg, warning Greg that Logan is morally bankrupt. The line has even more impact when you consider Brightstar is being accused of serious sexual misconduct against women. Ewan also told Greg: "There's a very persuasive argument to be made that Logan's worse than Hitler."

Season 2, Episode 8, "Dundee".
Written by Mary Laws.

Are your nips hard? They must be, you're so out in the cold.

***Roman**, to Shiv, after Logan accuses Shiv of disloyalty for considering the PGM position, even though Shiv suspects that Rhea Jarrell may be plotting to take over Waystar Royco.*

Season 2, Episode 7, "Return".
Written by Jonathan Glatzer.

HR says I'm the right guy for the job because it looks like I care, but I don't.

__Greg__, to Lukas Matsson, on whether Greg is a good person underneath. "I am," Greg responds. "It's just, ya gotta do what ya gotta do." Greg's transformation to the less-light side is complete.

Season 4, Episode 7, "Tailgate Party".
Written by Will Tracy.

If I lose, I want it correctly characterized as a huge victory.

Jeryd Mencken, *potential future president, tells Roman how he wants his election loss to be reported on Waystar's news channel, ATN. Mencken's line perfectly mirrors Donald Trump's baseless election fraud claims from the 2020 U.S. election.*

Season 4, Episode 8, "America Decides".
Written by Jesse Armstrong.

Everything's high risk if you're
a pussy.

Roman, *to Shiv, in front of Logan, Gerri and Karl,
as they discuss the fallout from Kendall's press
conference and Kendall's allegations against
Logan and Waystar Royco.*

Season 3, Episode 1, "Secession".
Written by Jesse Armstrong.

"

But then, who ends up king potato?

"

Tom, *to Shiv, over the phone, about which sibling would become Waystar CEO if the Roy children manage to unite and take Logan down together. Ultimately, Connor, Roman and Shiv agree that Kendall cannot win against Logan.*

Season 3, Episode 2, "Mass in Time of War".
Written by Jesse Armstrong.

If you jump out on someone on the road in the middle of the night, hit them on the head and shout, 'I'm not ambushing you,' it's still a fucking ambush.

Stewy, *to Logan and Gerri, after being told about Waystar's plans to acquire GoJo, a fact that Logan should have mentioned earlier but didn't due to its lack of "protein".*

Season 3, Episode 8, "Chiantishire".
Written by Jesse Armstrong.

"

It's like a private members club but for everyone... It's clickbait but for smart people.

"

__Roman__, describing his, Shiv and Kendall's new media start up, The Hundred, in a pitch for potential investors. Kendall chimes in with the meaningless: "We have the ethos of a nonprofit, but a path to crazy margins".

Season 4, Episode 1, "The Munsters".
Written by Jesse Armstrong.

31

> **"**
>
> What excited me about Jesse's script is that it wasn't about one family. It's more about the question of what happens when this kind of power is handed down through bloodlines, how does that affect the world around it? How does that affect the family members?
>
> **"**
>
> **Adam McKay**
> Variety, *January 11, 2018.*

66

You wanna do good things? Be a fucking nurse.

99

Logan, *to Kendall, after Kendall tells his father he believes Waystar could make more of a positive impact on the world. Insulting Kendall by telling him to become a nurse, statistically still a female role, was as precise and powerful as it was petulant.*

Season 1, Episode 10, "Nobody Is Ever Missing". Written by Jesse Armstrong.

I'm about to take a shit in your husband's mouth and I'm pretty sure he's going to tell me it tastes like coq au vin.

Lukas Matsson, to Shiv, after she learns that Matsson has over-inflated GoJo's subscriber numbers, a fact that poor Tom is going to have to deal with. Throughout Succession, food plays an important role – usually as an instrument to belittle and insult characters.

Season 4, Episode 7, "Tailgate Party".
Written by Will Tracy.

Oh, yeah, Tom. Tom of Siobhan.

***Oskar**, one of the GoJo executives, after being introduced to Tom in Norway for the acquisition talks. This killer introduction is precisely the kind of insult that plays on Tom's insecurities.*

Season 4, Episode 5, "Kill List".
Written by Jon Brown & Ted Cohen.

* "Yeah... and of ATN," Tom replies, albeit uncomfortably.

I'm sturdy. I'm a sturdy birdie…
Cock-a-doodle-doo!

Greg, *replying to Kendall, when asked
if Greg is a reliable asset that will not turn against
Kendall even if Logan demands he does. Greg's
response leaves Kendall to reply: "Say it three
times before the cock crows, motherfucker!"
before calling him "Big Bird" behind his back.*

Season 3, Episode 4, "Lion in the Meadow".
Written by Jon Brown.

66

Besides, everything might fall apart.
Kendall might go on a killing spree in
a 7-Eleven, and you might get your
dick stuck in an AI jerk machine.
I have to look out for myself.

99

Shiv, *to Kendall and Roman, on why she has to
keep her options open after Logan's health scare
and Kendall's bid for CEO. She's not wrong.*

Season 1, Episode 4, "Sad Sack Wasp Trap".
Written by Anna Jordan.

CHAPTER TWO

HOSTILE TAKEOVER

At the heart of this cutthroat family-(un)friendly comedy is the will of the individual members of the Roy family to win at all costs, all in the hope to claim the ultimate prize: the last laugh.

Thankfully for us, every character in *Succession* has the intellectual prowess to power-grab a quick-witted joke at someone else's expense, usually someone they dearly love underneath it all.

It's time to measure up and prepare for a hostile takeover of wit and wisdom and decide once and for all which character's quip is the biggest one to rule them all. Whose side are *you* on?

"
Underlined or crossed out?
"

Shiv, *to Kendall, regarding Logan's Will & Testament, and its ambiguous stance on Kendall as a replacement CEO. What isn't uncertain is Logan's desired headstone inscription: "Truthful lips endure forever but a lying tongue is but for a moment. (Proverbs 12:19)". Of course, this doesn't answer the question of what Greg's name was doing hiding in Logan's Will.*

Season 4, Episode 4, "Honeymoon States".
Written by Jesse Armstrong & Lucy Prebble.

* Jesse Armstrong revealed after the show ended that Kendall's name was indeed <u>underlined.</u>

"

Well, it sure as fuckin' shit doesn't say 'Shiv'.

"

Kendall, to Shiv, regarding Shiv's doubts that Logan's Will appoints Kendall as interim CEO after his death. Shiv's name is notable by its absence in the Will, despite being Logan's beloved only daughter.

Season 4, Episode 4, "Honeymoon States".
Written by Jesse Armstrong & Lucy Prebble.

Sure, they're young and they're fit, but they're European. They're soft, hammocked in their social security safety net, sick on vacation mania, and free healthcare. They may think they're Vikings, but we've been raised by wolves exposed to a pathogen that goes by the name Logan Roy and they have no idea what's coming to them. **99**

Gerri, *to the Waystar executives, before arriving in Norway for long and arduous merger talks with Matsson and his GoJo team. You can't help but feel it's an attack on the hardcore American work ethic as much as it is "soft" Europeans.*

Season 4, Episode 5, "Kill List".
Written by Jon Brown & Ted Cohen.

"

I read the script and fell in love with it. It was kind of loosely about the Murdochs — sort of a *King Lear*-meets-the-media-industrial-complex. When you finally come to a piece of work that you feel like you could really serve, and it would give you a chance as an actor to be fully expressed and fire on all cylinders, the stakes feel so high. I had to go fight for the role.

"

Jeremy Strong

GQ, November 27, 2018.

I fucking win. Oh, go on. Fuck off.
You nosy fucking pedestrians. 🙶🙶

Logan, *to Shiv, Kendall and Roman, after
Logan informs them that he and Caroline have
renegotiated a veto power clause in their divorce
agreement, effectively depriving the children
of company control after Logan decides to sell
Waystar without their knowing.*

Season 3, Episode 9, "All the Bells Say".
Written by Jesse Armstrong.

You better be smelling your fucking armpit, Romulus.

Logan, to Roman, as Roman starts to raise his hand during the vote of no confidence against Logan. Roman pussyed out when things got a little too tense in the boardroom and Logan refused to leave.

Season 1, Episode 6, "Which Side Are You On?".
Written by Susan Soon He Stanton.

66

Obviously, our public line will be that we are considering the offer, but it doesn't matter what you offer. He'll never recommend this to the board. You're gonna bleed cash. He's gonna bleed cash. It will never end. And maybe you'll kill him, but if you don't, he aims to kill you. He will go bankrupt or go to jail before he lets you beat him…

He will kill you on the business, and if that doesn't work, he will send people around. He will send men to kill your pets and fuck your wives, and it will never be over. So, that's the message. 99

Kendall, *to Sandy and Stewy, on Logan's perspective of their hostile takeover after Kendall pulled a dramatic U-turn following the death of Doddy.*

Season 2, Episode 1, "The Summer Palace".
Written by Jesse Armstrong.

Tell him that I'm gonna grind his fucking bones to make my bread.

Logan, *to Kendall's assistant Jess Jordan, after Kendall's shock-twist press conference, though Logan's enigmatic smile at the end of the Season 2 finale suggests he was actually proud of Kendall's defiance. In his eyes, Kendall was no longer curdled cream.*

Season 3, Episode 1, "Secession".
Written by Jesse Armstrong.

Life isn't a knight on horseback. It's a number on a piece of paper. It's a fight for a knife in the mud. **99**

Logan, *to Kendall, after Kendall suggests he "wants out" and to negotiate a billion-dollar pay-out from Waystar.*

Season 4, Episode 2, "Rehearsal".
Written by Tony Roche & Susan Soon He Stanton.

I'm worried about prison. I just feel because of my physical length, I could be a target for all kinds of misadventures.

Greg, *to Tom, on the prospect of time in prison in relation to the Brightstar Cruises scandal and trying to hook his "bauble of corporate wrongdoing" to one of Tom's branches.*

Season 3, Episode 6, "What It Takes".
Written by Will Tracy.

"

If it wasn't such a total fucking disaster, it would be a dream come true.

"

Tom, *to Caroline, about Shiv's pregnancy.*
A line as heart-breaking for Tom as it is
heart-melting for the viewer.

Season 4, Episode 9, "Church and State".
Written by Jesse Armstrong.

Stop ganging up on me like you're Lennon and McCartney and I'm George. I'm John, motherfuckers. He's still Connor... but he won having drinks with us at an auction.

Roman, *to Shiv and Kendall, about poor Connor not being allowed to be part of the band. The fact that Roman is about to break up the band and join with Logan once again to negotiate with Matsson in exchange for a position at ATN is pure John, not George.*

Season 4, Episode 2, "Rehearsal".
Written by Tony Roche & Susan Soon He Stanton.

I would like some suck-suck on my dicky dick.*

Connor, to Shiv, demanding favors in return for his signature to knock down Kendall's hostile take-over. The inappropriateness of this line – to his sister – is what makes it even more incredible.

Season 4, Episode 3, "The Disruption".
Written by Ted Cohen & Georgia Pritchett.

* "Same, I'm feeling brutally unsucky sucked," Roman responds.

What's it worth in terms of the me of it all?

Greg, to Logan, and what it's worth to him if he were to join Logan's side and get some legal counsel and protection under Waystar's legal team while he does it. The bumbling selfishness is pure Greg-esque.

Season 3, Episode 4, "Lion in the Meadow".
Written by Jon Brown.

Open the doors. Smells like the cheesemonger died and left his dick in the brie. I need to breathe.

__Logan__, to his family, describing the foul aroma of his Hampton house. It's pure poetry. The source of the smell was later revealed to be a bag of dead raccoons rotting in the fireplace, probably left by the contractors Logan had refused to pay.

Season 2, Episode 1, "The Summer Palace".
Written by Jesse Armstrong.

Nice vest, Wambsgans. It's so puffy. What's it stuffed with — your hopes and dreams?

Roman, to Tom, mocking Tom's preppy fashion style. Again. (Roman called Tom "a Transformer" in "Vaulter" for his "corporate boxy look", a way of making him feel inferior and not part of the family.)

Season 2, Episode 6, "Argestes".
Written by Jonathan Glatzer.

"

The baguette might be mightier than the bagel.

"

Greg, *to Tom and Lukas Matsson, on his opinion of "old lady France", deliberately wanting to sound stupid in a bid to stop Tom from intellectual humiliation at the hands of Matsson and his team.*

Season 4, Episode 5, "Kill List".
Written by Jon Brown & Ted Cohen.

66

I read Greg, and I was like,
'This is a guy that
makes sense to me,'
even though he makes no
sense at all as a guy.

99

Nicholas Braun
GQ, November 27, 2018.

Just text on your phone, ya bendy fuck.

Logan, *to Roman, in a scathing foreshadowing attack on the useless priorities of millennials, much like Roman. Roman, of course, gets the last laugh – or not – when he texts Logan a bendy dick pic in "Chiantishire", much to Logan's rage.*

Season 1, Episode 8, "Prague".
Written by Jon Brown.

Congratulations on saying the biggest number, you fucking morons.

Logan, *on the phone to Shiv, Roy and Ken, after he lost the Pierce bidding war to them and their $10 billion offer to Nan. In defeat, Logan weaponizes his words to destructive effect.*

Season 4, Episode 1, "The Munsters".
Written by Jesse Armstrong.

My grandpa made it clear that if
I want to secure my future then
I need to sever my links...
Negotiate a bit of a Grexit.

Greg, at a moral breaking point, asking "Uncle Loges", while in the toilet no less, about potentially leaving his Waystar role working for Tom to make "Grandpa Grumps" (Ewan) happy. It's a moment as hilarious as it is awkward, isn't it?

Season 2, Episode 8, "Dundee".
Written by Mary Laws.

66

I'd lay you badly, but I'd lay
you gladly.

99

Roman, to Gerri, as he flirts with his very-soon-
to-be boss alone in a hotel room as they wait for
news regarding Waystar's next CEO. (It's Gerri).
"Congratulations, you fucking bitch," Roman
says deadpan as soon as Gerri confirms the news
of her new role.

Season 3, Episode 1, "Secession".
Written by Jesse Armstrong.

You bust in here, guns in hand, and now you find they've turned to fucking sausages.

__Logan__, to Kendall, Roman, and Shiv, after Logan informs them that he and Caroline renegotiated their divorce agreement and a clause that would grant them veto power over any change in company control. Food, once again, is used to devastating effect.

Season 3, Episode 9, "All the Bells Say".
Written by Jesse Armstrong.

Well, Logan is very interested in what you're up to. You don't come home to us, you're gonna end up in a work camp. Logan is gonna fire a million poisonous spiders down your dickey. You better find an animal corpse to crawl into and hide.

Tom, *to Greg, over the phone, as he tries to ascertain where Greg's loyalties lie by using a penis metaphor. (A dickey, of course, is a formal shirtfront attached to a shirt collar and tucked into a waistcoat.)*

Season 3, Episode 2, "Mass in Time of War".
Written by Jesse Armstrong.

66

Can we be civil and not pull our guts out all over the table?

99

Logan, to Kendall, after Kendall demands a sit-down with his father over dinner to request a $2 billion buyout. Logan refuses. Kendall's emotional breakdown at the end of the episode lets the viewer know just how trapped Kendall feels.

Season 3, Episode 8, "Chiantishire".
Written by Jesse Armstrong.

You look like a dildo dipped in beard trimmings.

Roman, *to Stewy, about Stewy's designer beard stubble. The two have never been close, so Roman took the opportunity to unload his insults all over Stewy's face. Literally.*

Season 2, Episode 2, "Vaulter".
Written by Jon Brown.

> The truth is, I've been waiting thirty years for a show like this. It's comedy. It's tragic and it's shocking. It's like watching a trainwreck. My political orientation is on the left side of things, so any time I get to rub Fascists' noses in shit, I enjoy it in my own little way too.

Alan Ruck
Awards Daily, *June 21, 2019.*

Congratulations, Tom, I hear you
swallowed your own load.

Roman, *to Tom, after Tom's "hot" incident
with Tabitha at his own bachelor party,
organized by Roman. Tabitha later becomes
Roman's girlfriend.*

Season 1, Episode 8, "Prague".
Written by Jon Brown.

66

Well, these hands aren't gonna
fuck themselves so...

99

Roman, to Gil Eavis, after Roman gets into a
quarrel with the senator. This line was improvised
by actor Kieran Culkin.

Season 1, Episode 9, "Pre-Nuptial".
Written by Jesse Armstrong.

You're kinda like a peppy fun-gun set to MILF, with a Lean-In, woman-y branding thing that works with the Fitbit-moron-whatever people.

Roman, *degrading PGM CEO Rhea Jarrell, but in a way that also lets her know he thinks she's attractive. So, classic Roman, then.*

Season 2, Episode 8, "Dundee".
Written by Mary Laws.

Since the Roys first aired their dirty laundry in public, fans were quick to assume that the characters' names are meant to directly relate their personalities:

Kendall = Ken Doll
(completely emasculated by his father)

Shiv = A homemade knife
(perfect for backstabbing)

Roman = Roam-ing
(little substance and untethered to reality)

Connor = Con merchant
(deceiving people he is more than he is)

Tom = The everyman
(literally any old Tom, Dick, or Harry)

Greg = An egg
(fragile on the outside, but a mystery underneath the shell)

Logan = A wolverine
(fearless, but prone to fits of violence)

Look at you trying to get inside my head. Don't open Pandora's Box. There's just more dicks in there.

Roman, *to Gerri, after she asks him to stop sending her dick pics after Logan receives an eye-full by mistake. Roman doesn't like to be told no, even if it is by his boss-cum-work-wife.*

Season 3, Episode 8, "Chiantishire".
Written by Jesse Armstrong.

Okay, well, don't turn me into a word, Tom. I'm a guy. Why do you have all these little guys? These little Greggies running around? Who are these little Gregs?

Greg, to Tom, about the "mini-Gregs" and "Greglets" who are "Gregging" for Tom – much to Greg's disapproval. Or jealousy. Or both.

Season 4, Episode 3, "Connor's Wedding".
Written by Jesse Armstrong.

He didn't apologize when he hit our au pair with his car. 'It was her fault for being too short,' he said.

Roman, *describing rather brilliantly, in a nutshell, Logan, a man with obvious flaws but too successful to admit them unless it's a tactic for getting something else.*

Season 1, Episode 4, "Sad Sack Wasp Trap".
Written by Anna Jordan.

Well, we're making the right show.

Jesse Armstrong,
when he met the cast and crew for their initial read-through of the pilot script on US election day, November 2016, when Donald Trump won. Armstrong said it made writing a show about inherited power even more relevant.

Meh meh meh fucking meh...
Take it like a fucking man. You're
out. You're fucked. You tried to
kill me, but you failed. And you're
dead. Now fuck off!

Logan, *to Frank, after Kendall's no confidence*
vote showdown fails miserably.

Season 1, Episode 6, "Which Side Are You On?".
Written by Susan Soon He Stanton.

66

I mean if that wasn't a sign he was loco in the coco, I don't know what it is.

99

Kendall, *to Roman, about Logan's health, and his promise to make Roman the Chief Operating Officer of Waystar.*

Season 1, Episode 2, "Shit Show at the Fuck Factory".
Written by Tony Roche.

Is he nice? You're asking about the moral character of a man named Rat-fucker Sam? He's a fucking piece of fucking shit is what he is.

Tom, *to Greg, about Rat-fucker Sam, a Waystar employee whose job it is to dig up dirt on Waystar staff, at the request of executives and Logan. It was Sam who did a background check on Tom before he started dating Shiv.*

Season 2, Episode 3, "Hunting".
Written by Tony Roche.

"

Would you like to hear my favorite passage from Shakespeare? *Take the fucking money.*

"

Logan, to Nan Pierce, on Waystar's offer to buy Pierce Global Media, possibly referencing Shakespeare's famous passage about money: "He that wants money, means, and content is without three good friends." (As You Like It)

Season 3, Episode 5, "Retired Janitors of Idaho". Written by Tony Roche & Susan Soon He Stanton.

CHAPTER THREE

FILTHY LUCRE

For the Roy family, money makes their world go round until they get dizzy spinning on its power. But for these big business billionaires, money is boring without the influence to manipulate others.

From Greg's multi-million-dollar inheritance to Kendall's billion-dollar buyout, the GoJo merger to Royco buying presidents to keep deep in its pockets – and all the other deceits and receipts along the way, the Roy family's love of filthy lucre (they swear by it, literally) is the only thing keeping them from loving each other.

Here's the thing about being rich, okay? It's fucking great. It's like being a superhero, only better. You get to do what you want — the authorities can't really touch you. You get to wear a costume, but it's designed by Armani and it doesn't make you look like a prick.

Tom, *to Greg, about being rich. (And he's the poor one of the Roy family.)*

Season 1, Episode 6, "Which Side Are You On?". Written by Susan Soon He Stanton.

"

Who said I never killed anyone?

"

Kendall, *to Greg, hinting at his car accident in which the waiter Andrew Dodds (Doddy) died. Kendall said this line after Greg likened the press circus surrounding Kendall to that of the OJ Simpson case, before quickly clarifying: "I mean, if OJ never killed anyone."*

Season 3, Episode 1, "Secession".
Written by Jesse Armstrong.

> **"**
> I just adored every
> second playing the
> weird and wonderful
> human grease stain that
> is Tom Wambsgans.
> **"**

Matthew Macfadyen

*In his Golden Globes speech after winning
Best Supporting Actor, January 8, 2024.*

Go to the desert, dry yourself out. You have not been yourself. This could be the defining moment of your life. It'd eat everything. A rich kid kills a boy, you'd never be anything else. Or y'know, it could be what it should be: nothing at all. A sad, little detail at a lovely wedding where father and son are reconciled.

__Logan__, to Kendall, on how Kendall should handle his involvement in the death of the waiter Doddy at Shiv's wedding. The last line is a masterclass in manipulation, and all Kendall wanted to hear – not.

Season 1, Episode 10, "Nobody Is Ever Missing".
Written by Jesse Armstrong.

"

I blame myself. I spoiled you and now you're fucked. I'm sorry, you're a hothouse flower and you're nothing. You're curdled cream. Maybe you can write a book or, or collect sports cars or something, but for the world, no I'm sorry, you're not made for it. You can't stand it.

"

Logan, *to Kendall, about no longer having what it takes to be his rightful heir to the Waystar throne. Also, an insult to writers and car collectors everywhere.*

Season 1, Episode 10, "Nobody Is Ever Missing".
Written by Jesse Armstrong.

Karl, if your hands are clean, it's only because your whorehouse also does manicures.

Logan, to Karl, after Karl suggests himself for the CEO position when it becomes clear that Logan has to step back from the role for the GoJo merger. Nice try, Karl.

Season 3, Episode 1, "Secession".
Written by Jesse Armstrong.

Buckle up, fucklehead!

Tom, to Greg, after Greg snorts a lot of cocaine at Tom's bachelor party, even though he really didn't want to because Greg doesn't do "white drugs". Coke wasn't the only thing Tom consumed that night.

Season 1, Episode 8, "Prague".
Written by Jon Brown.

Greg the motherfucking Egg.
Look at you. You little Machiavellian
fuck.

Kendall, *to Greg, after Greg reveals that he
made copies of the Brightstar cruise scandal
documents as blackmail and leverage should he
take the fall for Tom's cover-up.*

Season 1, Episode 10, "Nobody Is Ever Missing".
Written by Jesse Armstrong.

> "

A lot of research went into *Succession*. I wrote the pilot solo, so there was a good deal of my own research and life experience in there. Then there's the writing room, which everyone informs with their stories and backgrounds. We thought of famous media families like the Hearsts, to modern-day Redstone, John Malone, Robert Fitz of Comcast, Murdoch, and Robert and Rebekah Mercer, who founded Breitbart. Lots of real-life moguls. We collected a myriad of these kinds of relationships that we knew about. And then like all creative people, you raid a surprising range of relationships that you've known from your own life.

"

Jesse Armstrong

In an interview with HBO.com by Laura Grainger.

"

This is why you don't hatch a plan with Connor, the first fucking pancake.

"

Shiv, *to her siblings, after Connor says he's starting to like Rhea Jarrell.*

Season 2, Episode 8, "Dundee".
Written by Mary Laws.

"

How about terror? Like, actual terror. Like a VR experience, but like, 'I'm actually gonna fucking die.' Like war.

"

Roman, *describing his pitch for a Waystar amusement park ride during his six-week management training in the Parks division where he is forced to play nice with the "normals". Later on, while dressed as the Dirk Turkey mascot, Roman utters the immortal line "I said, "'Gobbledy go fuck yourself!'" Amazing.*

Season 2, Episode 4, "Safe Room".
Written by Georgia Pritchett.

Your principles? Greg, don't be an asshole. You don't have principles.

Tom, *to Greg, after asking Greg to snoop into ATN inefficiencies so Tom can report directly to Logan.* For a second, Greg fools us into believing he has a moral compass, despite countering Tom's reply with: "I'm… against racism?"*

Season 2, Episode 2, "Vaulter".
Written by Jon Brown.

* ATN is, according to Tom, "Logan's G-spot.
I can finger-bang him all night long with a direct report."

"

He ate my fucking chicken. So,
what next? Stick his cock into my
potato salad?

"

Logan, to Shiv, about Tom, after Tom stole
Logan's chicken off his plate onboard the yacht
in a rare act of standing up for himself after that
disastrous congressional hearing and snapping
at Shiv (who had just insisted they continue their
open marriage with a threesome).

Season 2, Episode 10, "This Is Not for Tears".
Written by Jesse Armstrong.

The law? The law is people. And people is politics. And I can handle the people.

Logan, on refusing to cooperate with the Department of Justice's impending investigation into sexual misconduct. A metaphor, too, for Logan and his manipulative "handling" of his own family.

Season 4, Episode 3, "The Disruption". Written by Ted Cohen & Georgia Pritchett.

Death just feels very…one size fits all.

Roman, *succinctly summing up Logan's death, and how his father, an immortal, should have been somehow above it.*

Season 4, Episode 6, "Living+".
Written by Georgia Pritchett & Will Arbery.

66

I don't care what you think.
You're a tribute band.

99

Lukas Matsson, to Kendall and Roman,
following their visit to Norway to open the GoJo
merger talks. Roman getting a taste of his own
medicine. (See page 52.)

Season 4, Episode 5, "Kill List".
Written by Jon Brown & Ted Cohen.

> **"**
>
> To me, the stakes
> are life and death.
> I take Kendall as
> seriously as I take my
> own life.
>
> **"**

Jeremy Strong,
New Yorker, December 5, 2021.

Let's just keep one of his old sweaters. Less racist.

Shiv, to Roman, about retaining the Waystar Royco news channel, ATN, Logan's pride and joy. ATN has parallels to the right-wing conservative Fox News owned by the Murdoch family, the main inspiration for the Roy family.

Season 4, Episode 5, "Kill List".
Written by Jon Brown & Ted Cohen.

66

Benign fungus? Great title for your memoir.

99

Tom, *to Greg, cracking a joke about Greg's foot complaint, aboard the family's yacht.*

Season 2, Episode 10, "This Is Not for Tears".
Written by Jesse Armstrong.

The butter is too cold! The butter's all fucked! You're fuckwads and you fucked it! There's dinner rolls ripping out there as we speak!

Connor, *to the caterers of the RECNY Ball, the annual foundation fund-raiser gala hosted by the Roy family, about the too-cold-butter situation. Hardly the response of a presidential candidate in-waiting.*

Season 1, Episode 4, "*Sad Sack Wasp Trap*".
Written by Anna Jordan.

You're as fungible as fuck.

Logan, to Rhea, after she quits as CEO of
Waystar. The word fungible here is used
to meaning "replaceable". Logan's way of
weaponizing words strikes again!

Season 2, Episode 9, "DC".
Written by Jesse Armstrong.

You know, one waiter down, that makes sense. It took me forever to get a fucking drink at her wedding.

Roman, *in a callous remark to Kendall, after Shiv details the car accident that killed Doddy the waiter at her wedding. Roman's compassion for the poor "normals" reaches new lows.*

Season 3, Episode 9, "All the Bells Say".
Written by Jesse Armstrong.

I think the headline needs to be 'Fuck the weather, we're changing the cultural climate.'

Kendall, *on a post–press conference high, interrupts his new PR team's strategy presentation, with the heights of wanky pretension only Kendall can reach.*

Season 3, Episode 1, "Secession".
Written by Jesse Armstrong.

I'm not saying it's going to be the full Third Reich, but I am genuinely concerned that we could slide into a Russian Berlusconied Brazilian fuck pie.

Shiv, to Logan and Roman, after supporting the far-right Jeryd Mencken as the Republican nominee for president. Silvio Berlusconi was, of course, an Italian media mogul and prime minister who owned Mediaset, Italy's largest media company. Berlusconi never sold his personal assets of the company throughout his terms in office, to much controversy.

Season 3, Episode 6, "What It Takes".
Written by Will Tracy.

Fuck the patriarchy!

Kendall, *to the gathered press, on a red carpet. Never has a metaphor been meant so literally.*

Season 4, Episode 3, "The Disruption".
Written by Ted Cohen & Georgia Pritchett.

He can't do that. Fucking Pepsi doesn't just drop in to see Coke.

Kendall, *to Gerri, about rival Sandy Furness, of Furness Media, visiting the Waystar offices unscheduled and unannounced during the ongoing hostile takeover.*

Season 1, Episode 3, "Lifeboats".
Written by Jonathan Glatzer.

Wouldn't it be nice to just wake up in the morning and not feel like a fucking piece of shit? 99

Shiv, *to Nate Sofrelli, before they start their affair in an open marriage that Shiv insists Tom be one-third a part of.*

Season 1, Episode 6, "Which Side Are You On?".
Written by Susan Soon He Stanton.

You're going to sue Greenpeace? I like your style, Greg. Who do you think you are going to go after next? Save the Children?

Tom, *to Greg, after Greg's grandfather Ewan Roy leaves Greg's $250 million inheritance to Greenpeace because Greg went to work for his "Uncle Loges" at Waystar Royco.*

Season 3, Episode 5, "Retired Janitors of Idaho".
Written by Tony Roche & Susan Soon He Stanton.

I think Dad meant to say he wished Mom gave birth to a can opener, because at least then it would be useful.

Roman, *about Kendall, as the siblings argue about who should run the company in place of Logan while he's in hospital following his first health scare. The irony of this line coming from Roman is almost too much.*

Season 1, Episode 2, "Shitshow at the Fuck Factory".
Written by Tony Roche.

Fuck you too, you pusillanimous piece of fucking fool's gold – fucking, silver spoon asshole.

Stewy, *seething at Kendall, after Kendall reversed his position on his planned hostile takeover of Waystar Royco with Stewy and Sandy. Try to say this line five times fast.*

Season 2, Episode 1, "The Summer Palace".
Written by Jesse Armstrong.

I have no idea what you're talking about, but it sounds fucking slick, dude. Slicker than cum on a dolphin's back.

__Roman__, to Eduard Asgarov, the Azerbaijani billionaire, on Asgarov's plan to buy and flip a Scottish soccer team. Roman buys the Hearts (Heart of Midlothian), the team he thinks is Logan's favorite. It's actually the Hibs (Hibernian).

Season 2, Episode 9, "DC".
Written by Jesse Armstrong.

66

That's really wise. Hey, Buddha, nice Tom Fords.

99

Roman responds with an eye-roll to Kendall's pretentious philosophical remark: "In Buddhism, sometimes your greatest tormentor can also be your most perceptive teacher."

Season 4, Episode 2, "Rehearsal".
Written by Tony Roche & Susan Soon He Stanton.

CHAPTER FOUR

ENEMIES FOREIGN & DOMESTIC

The ruthlessly opportunistic Roy family are constantly fighting a war, first with each other – in no way a *civil* war – and, secondly, their enemies, foreign and domestic.

From ruthless sibling rivalries and marital strife at home to megalomaniacal Norwegians overseas, right-wing politicians to a bunch of embattled elitist executives, *Succession* is an all-out battleground, with every character struggling for survival from leaks, leverages and losing Logan's respect.

Who will be the last man, or woman, standing atop the rubble of Royco? There's only one way to find out…

I kinda always wondered if I was a psychopath, but apparently not. I'm actually relieved. We have to celebrate!

__Roman__, learning that no human deaths had occurred following the satellite launch explosion. More importantly, he discovers some depth to his soul. If only he felt the same way about poor Doddy.

Season 1, Episode 10, "Nobody Is Ever Missing". Written by Jesse Armstrong.

You disgusting little pig. You're pathetic. You are a revolting little worm, aren't you?... You little slime puppy.

__Gerri__, to the "over excited little boy" Roman, after much flirting on a phone call that ends with Gerri listening to Roman's "brilliance cascading". The line was improvised by J. Smith-Cameron and, no doubt, follows her everywhere she goes due to its now-iconic stature.

Season 2, Episode 4, "Safe Room".
Written by Georgia Pritchett.

"

You don't hear much about
syphilis these days. Very much the
MySpace of STDs.

"

Tom, *discussing Sandy Furness's suspected
syphilis, which turns him into "the angriest
fucking vegetable", to quote Stewy. We say
suspected – it was, of course, Gerri who spread
the rumor.*

Season 2, Episode 6, "Argestes".
Written by Susan Soon He Stanton.

Don't threaten me, Gerri. I don't have time to jerk off.

Roman, *to Gerri, after Gerri tells Roman to stick with her, and not his siblings, because "I'm an incredibly dangerous enemy." It was the happy ending Roman was seeking.*

Season 3, Episode 2, "Mass in Time of War".
Written by Jesse Armstrong.

Fuck you, plastic Jesus.

Shiv, to Kendall, after his about-turn press conference, an event Shiv would later call a "self-aggrandizing bullshit, a peacock fuckshow". If you say so, Shiv!

Season 3, Episode 2, "Mass in Time of War".
Written by Jesse Armstrong.

> **"**
>
> *L to the OG*
> *Dude be the OG*
> *A-N he playin'*
> *Playin' like a pro, see.*
>
> *L to the OG*
> *Dude be the OG*
> *A-N he playin'*
> *Playin' like a pro.*
>
> **"**

Kendall's rap in honour of Logan, at his birthday party. A performance so awkward it made Roman exclaim, "If I cringe any more I'll turn into a fossil."

The fucking Hercule Poirot of fucking piss over here.

Roman, to Tom, after Tom suggests Logan's been experiencing dementia from an untreated UTI for "quite some time". How Tom knows that is anyone's guess.

Season 3, Episode 5, "Retired Janitors of Idaho".
Written by Tony Roche & Susan Soon He Stanton.

66

I think you need to go and fuck yourself, and if I ever see you in the same room as Shiv again, I will pay men to break your legs. And if I got to jail – which I won't – so be it.

99

Tom, to Nate, after learning of his affair with Shiv on the day of their wedding, transforms from being an over-friendly host to passive-aggressive to downright aggressive as quickly as it takes Nate to put Tom's fucking wine back.

Season 1, Episode 10, "Nobody Is Ever Missing".
Written by Jesse Armstrong.

I just think if everyone's showing up to battle in armor, then I feel kind of exposed here in my loincloth. Sorry, bad visual.

Greg, *to his grandfather Ewan, after Ewan asks Greg why he may need independent legal representation if he hasn't done anything wrong after Kendall's press conference allegations.*

Season 3, Episode 2, "Mass in Time of War".
Written by Jesse Armstrong.

"
We are unusually subject to the
vicissitudes of public opinion.* **"**

*__Frank__, to Karl, putting the Waystar Royco
whistle-blower situation politely. (Vicissitudes is
another way of saying fluctuations, FYI.)*

Season 2, Episode 9, "DC".
Written by Jesse Armstrong.

* "Uh, I can translate. That's Frank for 'We're fucked',"
responds Karl.

125

81

The total number of
awards won by *Succession*
over its four-season run,
including:
19 Primetime Emmy Awards,
eight Critics Choice Awards,
nine Golden Globe Awards,
two Producers Guild of
America Awards, four Writers
Guild of America Awards, and
one Peabody Award.

Hey, if you wanna print something in your little book, you may print the following line: 'Connor Roy was interested in politics at a very young age.' That's it.

Connor, *to journalist Michelle Pantsil, keen as always to get across his own version of his life story for her biography – even if it's a life he's not lived.*

Season 2, Episode 4, "Safe Room".
Written by Georgia Pritchett.

66

The future is real, but... the past, well it's... all made up.

99

Logan, to Shiv, discussing the possibility of letting Rhea Jarrell take the fall for the Brightstar cruise scandal and implying that his past has always been defined by others seeking to rewrite history.

Season 2, Episode 8, "Dundee'.
Written by Mary Laws.

No c'mon, Tumbledown. He's your pal. Let's go see Hans Christian Anderfuck, see if he's been telling us fucking fairytales.

Logan, *to Roman, and Waystar executives, on the merger of equals, Waystar to Lukas Matsson. One of Logan's nicknames for Roman is "Tumbledown Dick" due to Roman's ambiguous sexuality.*

Season 3, Episode 9, "All the Bells Say".
Written by Jesse Armstrong.

Romulus, when you laugh, please do it at the same volume as everyone else. We didn't get you from a hyena farm.

Logan, *to Roman, on Roman's displeasing social manners to Logan's ears. (FYI, Romulus was the first mythical king of Rome, and one who killed his twin Remus for the role in an act of sibling rivalry that would make even Roman blush.)*

Season 2, Episode 5, "Tern Haven".
Written by Will Tracy.

Bring him up in the dumbwaiter like a fucking hamburger.

Logan, *about Kendall, who makes an unexpected appearance at the Waystar offices. The dumbwaiter could also be a smart reference to Doddy, the waiter who spilled champagne on Logan at Shiv and Tom's wedding, who got kicked out, only to be befriended by Kendall.*

Season 4, Episode 3, "The Disruption".
Written by Ted Cohen & Georgia Pritchett.

I gots the ol' rumblin' tum.

Greg, *speaking with his grandfather Ewan and telling him that he was hungry before they hit the road. It's the most awkward small talk ever seen on screen.*

Season 1, Episode 5, "I Went to Market".
Written by Georgia Pritchett.

You know who drinks milk?
Kittens and perverts.

*__Roman__, when quizzed by Logan about how
much a gallon of milk costs, without knowing
the answer. Do perverts drink milk?
Answers on a postcard, please.*

Season 2, Episode 3, "Hunting".
Written by Tony Roche.

So, this is what you do? You, like, go to a club, and then you come to, like, this other part where the club sort of isn't?

Greg, to Tom, awkwardly describing the ridiculous concept of a VIP section, a place he'd clearly never been to before. Next time you're in a VIP section, this is how you'll describe it.

Season 1, Episode 6, "Which Side Are You On?".
Written by Susan Soon He Stanton.

Roi

Jesse Armstrong used the surname Roy for his lead characters as Roi, in French, translates to "King".

Everyone has a plan until they get punched in the mouth.

Shiv, to Kendall and Roman, regarding the plan for Waystar's deal with GoJo and Lukas Matsson. These famous words were spoken originally by legendary boxer Mike Tyson.

Season 4, Episode 5, "*Kill List*".
Written by Jon Brown & Ted Cohen.

It was supposed to be choreographed. That's about as choreographed as a dog getting fucked on roller skates.

Logan, to Hugo, on the botched approach to the Pierce family. This episode – and perhaps specifically the delivery of this line – earned Brian Cox his first Emmy nomination for the show in 2020.

Season 2, Episode 3, "Hunting".
Written by Tony Roche.

You're a good guy. You're my best pal. I mean, what are people? What are people? They're economic units. I'm a hundred feet tall, these people are pygmies. But together they form a market. What is a person? It has values, aims... but it operates in a market.

Logan, *to his bodyguard, Colin, during Waystar's annual foundation gala, questioning the market value of people.*

Season 1, Episode 4, "Sad Sack Wasp Trap".
Written by Anna Jordan.

We are bullshit. You are bullshit. You're fucking bullshit, I'm fucking bullshit. She's bullshit. It's all fucking nothing. I'm telling you this because I know it. We're nothing.

Roman, *to Kendall and Shiv, finding a moment of clarity about himself and his family as the end of the show draws near.*

Season 4, Episode 10, "With Open Eyes".
Written by Jesse Armstrong.

This is not the end. I'm gonna build something better. Something faster, lighter, leaner, wilder. And I'm gonna do it from in here with you lot! You're fucking pirates!

__Logan__ gives an impassioned speech to the workers of ATN after retaining the news channel in the GoJo merger. It's his last big speech before his sudden death.

Season 4, Episode 2, "Rehearsal".
Written by Tony Roche & Susan Soon He Stanton.

66

I don't do white drugs.

99

***Greg**, to Kendall, unsuccessfully trying to turn down Kendall's offer to do "a chunk of chang" with him after admitting Logan sent him to spy on Kendall. It's Greg, however who, in Tom's words, ends up the "greedy coke whore" after gobbling up the cocaine.*

Season 1, Episode 8, "Prague".
Written by Jon Brown.

He could say anything.
He could tell everyone he's
Barbra Streisand.

Shiv, *about Logan, after Logan begins
acting strangely because of a suspected UTI.*

Season 3, Episode 5, "Retired Janitors of Idaho".
Written by Tony Roche & Susan Soon He Stanton.

"

I'm not a radical feminist, Dad, but I think perhaps we should not fire her for receiving pictures of my dick.

"

Roman, *to Logan, after sending Gerri, and Logan (accidently), selfies of his penis. Logan's anger at Roman's photography perhaps stems not from the images themselves but from Gerri and Roman's strange alliance, a threat to Logan's power after he named Gerri CEO.*

Season 3, Episode 8, "Chiantishire".
Written by Jesse Armstrong.

You love showing your pee-pee
to everyone but someday you're
actually gonna have to fuck
something.

*__Shiv__, ridiculing Roman's sexual dysfunction
while the siblings have a strategy meeting in
Kendall's daughter's bedroom. After Roman
storms out, Kendall tells Shiv it wasn't that harsh
an insult: "He loves it. He'll be out there jerking
off wearing my ex-wife's panties."*

Season 3, Episode 2, "Mass in Time of War".
Written by Jesse Armstrong.

We were thinking of murdering you. But, you know, it's too much prep. Too much murder admin.

Shiv, *to Kendall, after the three siblings agree Kendall should become CEO after the GoJo merger in a rare moment of unity between them. Of course, moments later, Shiv changes her mind.*

Season 4, Episode 10, "With Open Eyes".
Written by Jesse Armstrong.

CHAPTER FIVE

FLESH & BLOOD

Succession is all about keeping it in the family, even if that means the family destroys itself in the process. And, in that respect, the Roy family are just as dysfunctional as the rest of us, no different despite the power, fame, fortune and never-ending supply of whirly birds.

While the Roys work hard to sacrifice everything they have for the sake of each other – despite, and to spite, each other – *Succession* shows us time and again that the bad blood that so often runs in families is still thicker than water, no matter how many black sheep there may be…

"

Family, Siobhan! If you don't
understand that, then fuck off!

"

Logan, *to Shiv, accusing Shiv of disloyalty
for considering the PGM position offered by
Rhea Jarrell. Of course, Logan decrying the
importance of family when he too uses his family
like pawns in a game of chess is a bit rich.
And there's none richer than Logan.*

Season 2, Episode 7, "Return".
Written by Jonathan Glatzer.

The good thing about having a family that doesn't love you is you learn to live without it. 🙶🙶

__Connor__, about his family, during his heart-breaking wedding rehearsal speech. It's at this moment that the viewer realizes that Connor is the only one who understands that Shiv, Kendall and Roman will never get anything more than money from Logan. Connor's learned to live without love from his family because he's realized they're all too busy chasing after Logan's approval and shave topped caring for each other.

Season 4, Episode 2, "Rehearsal".
Written by Tony Roche & Susan Soon He Stanton.

After the show's first season was aired, life began to imitate art.

Global multinational AT&T acquired Time Warner, HBO's parent company, in a high-profile and controversial merger that mirrored *Succession*'s botched Pierce deal and the GoJo merger.

The truth is that my father is a malignant presence, a bully, and a liar, and he was fully personally aware of these events for many years and made efforts to hide and cover up… the notion that he would have allowed millions of dollars in settlements and compensation to be paid without his explicit approval is utterly fanciful.

Kendall, *in his testimony to the DOJ, where he was set to accept responsibility for the company's handling of the Brightstar sexual misconduct crimes, but ultimately takes a different direction.*

Season 2, Episode 10, "This Is Not for Tears".
Written by Jesse Armstrong.

All those years blaming yourself for Rose? That really wasn't your fault. This, though? This is your fault. This empire of shit. Time to pay up.

Ewan, *to Logan, mentioning their baby sister Rose, who died young from polio, before sticking the knife in with a killer blow.*

Season 2, Episode 8, "Dundee".
Written by Mary Laws.

66

Roman's a knucklehead, Shiv's a fake, Kenny is screwy. Why can't I get a shot?

99

Connor, *summing up his siblings in a nutshell (and perhaps the one and only time Connor made any practical sense), after pleading with Logan to give him a job as head of Waystar's European cable division, a role he considers to be "nothing vital", probably to Logan's dismay, if he wasn't so preoccupied with taking a piss.*

Season 3, Episode 5, "Retired Janitors of Idaho". Written by Tony Roche & Susan Soon He Stanton.

Look, if we come through this...
is there a thing where we like...
talk to each other about stuff?
Normally?

Roman, *to Kendall and Shiv, onboard the yacht,
hoping for a human connection with his siblings
once the Brightstar scapegoat is found.
Roman is mocked by Kendall and Shiv. "How am
I the mature one here?" he concludes.*

Season 2, Episode 10, "This Is Not for Tears".
Written by Jesse Armstrong.

Dad, you beat Roman with a fucking slipper in Gustav 'til he cried for ordering lobster, remember? And Kendall tries to kill you and he's five minutes out in the cold?

Shiv, *in "family therapy" with Logan, discussing Logan letting Kendall off too easily after his doomed hostile takeovers.*

Season 2, Episode 1, "The Summer Palace".
Written by Jesse Armstrong.

66

I'd like to welcome Tom to the
family; I don't feel like I'm losing a
sister. I don't feel like I'm gaining
a brother, either. I don't feel
anything. It's a mental disorder.
it's called borderline personality
disorder. Why is everybody
laughing? What can I tell you about
Tom? Very little, nothing really
sticks. He was born and grew up,
in, um, America. The middle. In
an Applebee's. I should imagine.

I've never asked. His parents are here. I'd point them out but they're basically nobodies. What? Folks, I don't want to be mean – it's what a best man's speech is. They're actually incredibly lovely people. Just poor and uninteresting. **99**

__Roman__, about Tom, punching down during his best man's speech discussing Tom's move from Midwestern nobody to a coastal elite. An awkward affair, to put it mildly.

Season 1, Episode 10, "Nobody Is Ever Missing". Written by Jesse Armstrong.

Where are your kids? Where's all your kids, Uncle Logan? On your big birthday?

__Greg__, roasting Logan, but taking it a little too far even though birthday boy Logan asked for it. Not many in Logan's circle could get away with saying something so cruel, but Greg – with his bumbling, unthreatening charm – gets away with it. And what a brutal line to an old man on his birthday.

Season 4, Episode 1, "The Munsters".
Written by Jesse Armstrong.

66

He died fishing his iPhone from a clogged toilet... He was a man who wasn't wearing his compression socks so he could look hot for Kerry.

99

Tom, *to Greg, about the moment of Logan's passing, digging his phone out from a jet toilet thought to be clogged by Karl. But it's so out of character for Logan, surely it can't be true?*

Season 4, Episode 4, "Honeymoon States". Written by Jesse Armstrong & Lucy Prebble.

Oh, let's not pretend, Shiv? This isn't about Dad. This is because you like the power. It gets you close to the poles you like to grease. And, Rom, you couldn't get a job in a fucking burger joint let alone a Fortune 500 without some nepotism. And, Con, you like the glamour it gives to a fucking freak in the desert.

__Kendall__'s emotional meltdown merges power, money, nepotism, his siblings, and, as always, Logan.

Season 1, Episode 10, "Nobody Is Ever Missing".
Written by Jesse Armstrong.

I think you are incapable of love.
And I think you are maybe not a
good person to have children with.

Tom, *to a secretly pregnant Shiv at their pre-election party. Intrigued to see how Tom gets out of this one.*

Season 4, Episode 7, "Tailgate Party".
Written by Will Tracy.

66

Intrigued to see how he gets out of
this one.

99

Shiv, *about Logan, at Logan's funeral.*

Season 4, Episode 9, "Church and State".
Written by Jesse Armstrong.

Nothing matters, Ken. Nothing fucking matters. Dad's dead and the country's just a big pussy waiting to get fucked.

__Roman__, to Kendall, spiraling at the state of play as the election results – and his impending future – draw near.

Season 4, Episode 8, "America Decides".
Written by Jesse Armstrong.

> "

Shiv loves Tom, but doesn't know how to. She doesn't know how to do a relationship that isn't transactional.

"

Sarah Snook
Rolling Stone, *April 9, 2023.*

66

Dad sounds amazing. I would have liked to have met Dad.

99

Shiv, *about Logan, after reading the lies about how great Logan was in the press following his death.*

Season 4, Episode 4, "Honeymoon States".
Written by Jesse Armstrong & Lucy Prebble.

I don't think I'm a very good father. Maybe the poison drips through.

Kendall, *to Shiv, about his own relationship with his children, as Kendall decides his fate: side with Roman and destroy his own family or choose his kids and lose the company to Matsson.*

Season 4, Episode 8, "America Decides".
Written by Jesse Armstrong.

It's not my fault that you didn't get his approval. I have given you endless approval and it doesn't fill you up because you're broken.

Tom, *to Shiv, their bitter clearing of the air ends with Tom dropping the biggest of all truth bombs. Siobhan's response: "I don't like you."*

Season 4, Episode 7, "Tailgate Party".
Written by Will Tracy.

Like, is that even true? Or is that like, a new position or a tactic?

Tom, *to Shiv, his response after Shiv tells him she's pregnant with his child. Tom's initial response speaks volumes of the calculating and mistrust within the relationship, but this is the first time it is verbalized so precisely.*

Season 4, Episode 8, "America Decides".
Written by Jesse Armstrong.

What we do today will always be what we did the day our father died. So, let's grieve, and whatever, but not do anything that restricts our future freedom of movement.

__Kendall__, to Shiv and Roman, about the importance of how they respond to Logan's death. Time magazine described this moment the best: Are they monsters trying to behave like humans or humans trying to convince themselves they're tough enough to be monsters?

Season 4, Episode 3, "Connor's Wedding".
Written by Jesse Armstrong.

You've fallen in love, finally. You've fallen in love with our scheduling opportunities.

Tom, *to Shiv, on having a relationship breakthrough with his pregnant wife, after Tom is announced as new CEO of Waystar Royco. When Shiv then asks Tom if he would be interested in a "real relationship", Tom's answer is noncommittal. Finally, he has all the power.*

Season 4, Episode 10, "With Open Eyes".
Written by Jesse Armstrong.

I wouldn't have missed this for the world. This is a very memorable day. A day I'll never forget, as long as I live. I wanted it to be perfect. For my daughter. And it is. Nothing could ruin this. It means so much to be surrounded by everyone we love and trust and hold dear. Because nothing is more important than family.

Logan, in his father-of-the-bride speech, talking about his beloved "Pinky" but looking squarely at Kendall throughout.

Season 1, Episode 10, "Nobody Is Ever Missing".
Written by Jesse Armstrong.

"

I'm better than you. I hate to say this because I love you, but you're kind of evil.

"

Kendall, to Logan, over that awkward dinner. The word "better" doing a lot of heavy lifting, considering Kendall "wants out" of the family empire when Logan knows he really doesn't.

Season 3, Episode 8, "Chiantishire".
Written by Jesse Armstrong.

2.9 million

The total number of viewers who watched *Succession*'s final episode, an increase in 68 per cent from the Season 3 finale.

Ahead of the fourth-season premiere, *Succession* had been watched for more than half a billion minutes across all streaming platforms.

66

You would never have dared not to come to his funeral when he was alive.

99

Shiv, to Tom, for daring to miss Logan's funeral. Tom's response is killer: "The thing about your dad is that he's lost quite a lot of influence over the past few days." Boom!

Season 4, Episode 9, "Church and State".
Written by Jesse Armstrong.

"

Oh, you're sick with grief?
You might wanna put down that
fish taco. You're getting your
melancholy everywhere.

"

*__Gerri__, to Tom, who scolds Tom for his arguably
unbelievable response to Logan's sudden death.*

Season 4, Episode 3, "Connor's Wedding".
Written by Jesse Armstrong.

You're needy love sponges. And I'm a plant that grows on rocks and lives off insects that die inside of me. If Willa doesn't come back that's fine. Because I don't need love. It's like a superpower. And if she comes back and doesn't love me, that's okay too, 'cause I don't need it.

__Connor__, to his siblings, at the karaoke parlor, after Connor sang, aptly, Leonard Cohen's "Famous Blue Raincoat". Is this wonderful speech more hyperbolic melodrama… or the truth?

Season 4, Episode 3, "Connor's Wedding".
Written by Jesse Armstrong.

"

Oh, man. He never even
liked me.

"

__Connor__, to Shiv and Kendall, immediately after
he is told that Logan is probably dead. Chilling
words from the first fucking pancake and a
succinct summary of the first-born's relationship
with his father.

Season 4, Episode 3, "Connor's Wedding".
Written by Jesse Armstrong.

"

What? No, no, I can't have that.

"

Shiv, to Kendall, reacting immediately to the news that Logan is probably dead. Her choice of words is apt: Daddy's spoiled little girl finally gets something she doesn't want.

Season 4, Episode 3, "Connor's Wedding".
Written by Jesse Armstrong.

He made me hate him, and then he died. I feel like he didn't like me. I disappointed him.

***Kendall**, to Frank, about Logan's opinion of him, mirroring how Connor believed Logan felt about him – that he simply wasn't liked or respected by his own father, even though he was loved.*

Season 4, Episode 4, "Honeymoon States".
Written by Jesse Armstrong & Lucy Prebble.

Yes, if it is to be said, so it be,
so it is.

Greg, *when asked by Senator Eavis at a
Senate Hearing if he was Tom's assistant.
Greg's flubbed response prompts Eavis to tell
Greg: "You can speak to us normally."*

Season 2, Episode 9, "DC".
Written by Jesse Armstrong.

> "
>
> The first thing I asked Jesse Armstrong was 'Does Logan love his children?' He said, "Yeah, he really loves his children.' It's about trying to reclaim that love. They've just never learned how to deal with their entitlement.
>
> "

Brian Cox
Variety, June 13, 2023.

If Dad didn't need me right now,
I don't exactly know what I would
be for.

Kendall, *confides to Shiv his belief that his
loyalty to Logan is all he is worth.*

Season 2, Episode 4, "Safe Room".
Written by Georgia Pritchett.

"

Well, of course, it's a fucking minus! I didn't make the world!

"

Logan, to Shiv, about being a woman in a man's world. The truth, of course, is that Logan is powerful enough to remake the world in her image – but chooses not to.

Season 2, Episode 2, "Vaulter".
Written by Jon Brown.

I think a lot of the time, I'm really pretty unhappy. I wonder if the sad I'd be without you would be less than the sad I get from being with you.

Tom, *to Shiv, about their ongoing on-off happiness. It's one of the show's most poignant and universally adored lines, delivered by a tender Tom in a moment of brutal honesty.*

Season 2, Episode 10, "This Is Not for Tears".
Written by Jesse Armstrong.

66

I can't forgive you. But it's okay and I love you.

99

Kendall, to Logan, his last words to his father,
showing (perhaps, genuinely, for the first time)
that underneath his constant pathetic desire for
Logan's love, Kendall does have the strength to
stand up to his brutal father.

Season 4, Episode 3, "Connor's Wedding'.
Written by Jesse Armstrong.

You're my boy. You're my
number one boy.

Logan, *to Kendall, during a rare moment of
genuine (?) affection, following the aftermath of
Kendall's car crash and the death of Doddy, the
waiter. Proof, perhaps, that Logan does indeed
put numerical units of preference upon his
children.*

Season 1, Episode 10, "Nobody Is Ever Missing".
Written by Jesse Armstrong.

Now people might want to tend and prune the memory of him to denigrate that force. That magnificent, awful force of him, but my God, I hope it's in me.

Kendall, *about Logan, during Logan's funeral, concluding what the viewer has known all along: that he is truly his father's son.*

Season 4, Episode 9, "Church and State".
Written by Jesse Armstrong.

You're marrying a man fathoms beneath you because you don't want to risk being betrayed. You're a fucking coward.

Logan, _to Shiv, about her upcoming marriage to Tom. Ironically, when Tom "wins" the CEO role at the end of the show, Tom finally becomes Shiv's social equal – though how long that lasts after the credits roll is anyone's guess._

Season 1, Episode 7, "Austerlitz".
Written by Lucy Prebble.

I think I've contextualized it... I just like, OK, you know, if I'm the king and you're the queen, maybe it's fine to... fuck the odd peasant.

Tom, *to Shiv, trying to make himself believe that he agrees to their open marriage, when clearly all he wants is to love and be loved by Shiv. Terms and conditions apply.*

Season 2, Episode 2, "Vaulter".
Written by Jon Brown.

> "I've been acting for 60 years, but now I am the 'fuck off' man. It has its charm. But it's not easy to be a cultural icon. As they say in Scotland, it's an awfully big job for an ordinary boy."

Brian Cox
Variety, June 13, 2023.

❝

It's war! Fuck off!

❞

Logan, to Frank, after Frank suggests
Logan cooperate with the authorities after
Kendall's press conference and he spills the
beans on Waystar Royco.

Season 3, Episode 1, "Secession".
Written by Jesse Armstrong.

I did my best. And whenever you fucked up, I cleaned up your shit. And I'm a bad person? Fuck off, kiddo.

__Logan__, to Kendall, during their dinner where Kendall requests a $2 billion buyout. No one, not even Logan presumably, assumes that he truly believes he did his best.

Season 3, Episode 8, "Chiantishire".
Written by Jesse Armstrong.